There's More Than One Way to Eat!
A My Tubey Book

Written and Illustrated by

Rhiannon Merritt-Rubadue

ISBN-13: 978-1461065739
ISBN: 1461065739

THANKS
To my husband. You did it again!

There are many ways to eat, more than you may know.

We all need healthy food, so we can learn and grow!

Many of my friends can eat food with their mouths—

but some eat in a special way, that we can learn about!

This is my friend, Kendall.  She is almost one.

Sometimes she drinks a bottle,

but sometimes she drinks none.

When her tummy isn't feeling well,

but she needs to eat some food,

her daddy pushes special milk,

through something called an NG-tube.

This tube tapes to her face and tucks behind her ear.

It goes through her nose and down her throat,

so food can get inside of her!

Now she can eat, now she can grow!

Now I'd like you to meet Jackson,

he throws-up a lot.

He has a sickness called reflux

so he doesn't want to eat a drop.

To be strong enough for soccer,

he needs to get some food!

Please don't worry for him—

he has a G-tube!

If he lifts up his shirt

you can see it there.

It doesn't keep him from playing

and he can go anywhere.

His G-tube is like a little hose

that goes into his stomach.

It has a hole for squirting food

and it doesn't hurt a bit.


Now he can eat, now he can grow!

Your stomach isn't the only place

you can put your food.

This is Delaney,

whose small intestine holds her feeding tube.

Since she can't have food inside her tummy

and she still needs a way to eat,

Her doctor put in a J-tube,

and it's actually pretty neat!

Right below the stomach, the small intestine begins.

It takes nutrients from your food, from the beginning to the end.

The J-tube looks like a G-tube, and has the same little hole.

Food goes right inside it, keeping Delaney full.

Now she can eat, now she can grow!

## Jejunal Feeding Tube

junum/small intestine

tube

balloon

tube

Jejunum/small intestine

skin

skin

Button style tube

valve/opening

plug

Stomach

J-tube

small intestine

Bo can't have food in his tummy or intestines,

so where can it go?

You might not believe it,

but his blood-vessels can help him grow!

What a perfect place to put your food

when your tummy doesn't work,

TPN is what it's called,

and no, it doesn't hurt.

A special tube goes in your chest, right into your veins,

it can give you nutrients, each and every day.

Just take a look at Bo!

Now he can eat, now he can grow!

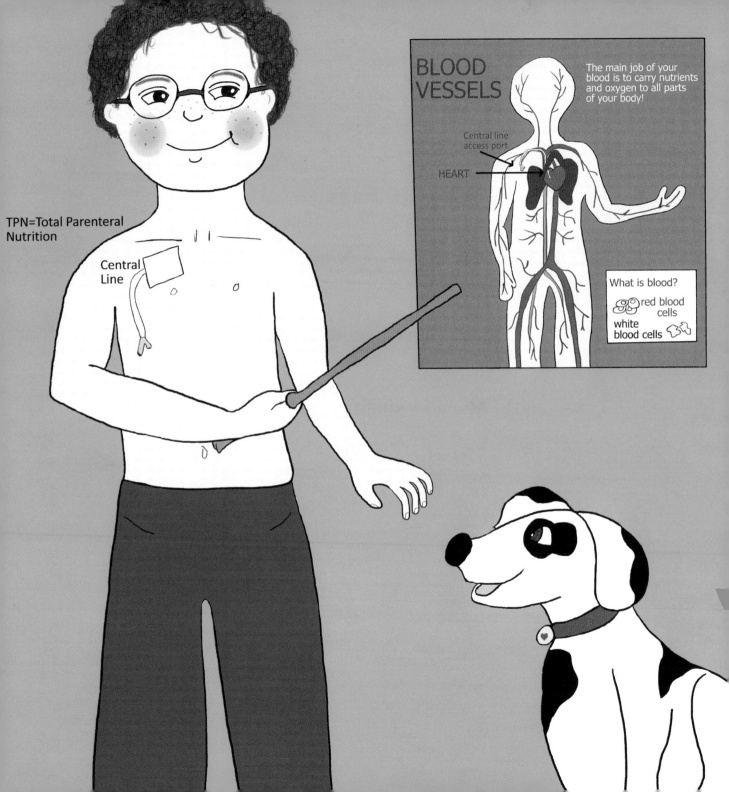

Lots of kids have feeding tubes, maybe you have one, too!

No matter how you get your food,

children everywhere eat and grow,

just the same as you!

# TUBE FEEDING GLOSSARY

**AMT Mini ONE® Button**: A type of low-profile G-tube, J-tube, or GJ-tube. Sits closer to the body so is less noticeable and great for active children. Manufactured by Applied Medical Technology, Inc.

**Blenderized Diet**: An alternative to canned enteral formulas, using real foods that you prepare yourself at home, blend with a high powered blender, and deliver via feeding tube.

**Bolus**: A method of tube feeding that delivers a large amount of food over a short period of time, similar to typical eating patterns. It allows freedom of movement so the child isn't tethered to a feeding bag for long periods, but may not be tolerated by all children.

**Central Line**: A central venous catheter, also called a central line, is a long thin, flexible tube used to give medicines, fluids, nutrients, or blood products over a long period of time, usually several weeks or more. A catheter is often inserted in the arm or chest through the skin into a large vein. The catheter is threaded through this vein until it reaches a large vein near the heart.

**Cream**: Referring to barrier creams that may help with an irritated stoma area, such as Calmoseptin, Triamcinolone Acetonide Cream, or OTC cortisone creams.

**Esophagus**: A long muscular tube that moves food from the mouth to the stomach.

**Extension set**: Tubing that you attach during tube feeding, between your feeding tube and your syringe or feeding pump. These sets allow complete range of motion by rotating within the feeding port during movement.

Feeding pump: A programmable electronic pump that can disperse formula, TPN, or blenderized foods at a rate and volume of your choosing during tube feeds.

Feeding tube: A feeding tube is a medical device used to provide nutrition to patients who cannot obtain nutrition by mouth. The state of being fed by a feeding tube is called gavage, enteral feeding or tube feeding. A variety of feeding tubes are used in medical practice. They are usually made of polyurethane or silicone. They are classified by site of insertion and intended use and include NG-tubes, G-tubes, GJ-tubes, J-tubes, TJ-tubes, and GE-tubes.

Granulation Tissue: Pink or red, bumpy tissue around the tube/stoma. Bleeds easily and may create mucous.

Gravity Feed: A method of tube feeding whereby a large syringe vessel is filled with formula, attached via extension set to the feeding tube, and suspended above the child to flow freely with no help from a pump. A caregiver can adjust the height of the syringe to adjust the rate of flow.

G-tube: Refers to a Gastrostomy. This is a surgically placed feeding tube placed directly into the stomach.

Jejunum: The jejunum is the middle part of the small intestine extending from the duodenum to the ileum. It is responsible for digestion.

J-tube: Refers to a Jejunostomy. This is a surgically placed feeding tube placed directly into the small intestine, ending in the Jejunum. There can also be a GJ-tube which has ports for both the stomach and the intestine.

**MIC-KEY Button**: A type of low-profile G-tube, J-tube, or GJ-tube. Sits closer to the body so is less noticeable and great for active children. Manufactured by Kimberly-Clark.

**NG-tube**: Refers to a Naso-Gastric feeding tube. It is inserted into the nose, passes through the esophagus, and down to the stomach.

**Pack**: Refers to a small backpack that can hold a feeding pump, a bag of formula, and an ice-pack. It is worn on the back while the child is being tube fed and gives the child greater mobility so she can play!

**PEG Tube**: Often the first G-tube that is placed, and is replaced several months later with a low-profile G-tube. PEG stands for percutaneous endoscopic gastronomy.

**Small Intestine**: The small intestine is about 15-20 feet long and is made up of three sections: the duodenum, the jejunum and the ileum. The majority of digestion and absorption from food happens here.

**Stoma**: An opening from inside to outside the body. G-tubes, J-tubes, and TPN create a stoma via their channel into the body.

**Syringe**: Tube feeders have syringes that are specially designed to fit together with feeding tubes and their extension sets so you can administer medications, formula, blenderized foods, and water either by gravity feed, or by pushing it in.

**TPN**: Refers to Total Parenteral Nutrition, which bypasses the digestive system and delivers nutrients intravenously. TPN is used when individuals cannot or should not get their nutrition by eating.

# CONDITIONS THAT MAY REQUIRE A FEEDING TUBE IN CHILDREN

Arthrogryposis Multiplex Congenita
Aspiration
Brain Injury
Cancer
Celiac Disease
Chromosome Disorders
Cystic Fibrosis
Eosinophilic Disorders
Food Allergies
GERD (Gastroesophogeal Reflux Disease)
Heart Conditions
Hiatal Hernia
Mitochondrial Disease
Motility Disorders
Prematurity
Rare Diseases
Respiratory Conditions
Structural Abnormalities
Unknown Diseases/disorders

# MORE BOOKS FROM THE MY TUBEY SERIES

My Tubey: A Day in the Life of a Tube Fed Boy (Available)
978-1460964651, $12.99 paperback (www.MyTubeyBooks.com to order)

My Tubey: A Day in the Life of a Tube Fed Girl (Available)
978-1460923085, $12.99 paperback (www.MyTubeyBooks.com to order).

Bye-Bye Tubey: It's Time to Remove My Tube! (Coming soon!)
If your child has a date set for removing his or her feeding tube, it can be a scary prospect. After all, their tubey has become a part of their body and now it's going to be removed! Help ease their anxiety and fear with this informative, colorful book that shows a child going to the doctor with mom to get her tubey taken out.

My Tubey Goes to Preschool (Coming soon!)
Follow along as a tube fed child goes to preschool and plays with new friends! Full-color illustrations address the challenges of being tube fed at school.

# HELPFUL RESOURCES

- **www.MyTubeyBooks.com**
- www.nutritioncare.org
  - A.S.P.E.N.: American Society for Parenteral and Enteral Nutrition
- www.babycenter.com
  - Support forum: search for "Babies and Children with a Feeding Tube"
- www.blenderizeddiet.com
- www.BundieBaby.com
- www.cdhnf.org
  - Children's Digestive Health and Nutrition Foundation
- www.FeedingEssentials.com
- www.feedingtubeawareness.com
- www.feeding-underweight-children.com
- www.iffgd.org
  - International Foundation for Functional Gastrointestinal Disorders
- www.infantrefluxdisease.com
- www.mitoaction.org (MitoAction)
- www.mybuttonbuddies.com
- www.naspghan.org
  - North American Society for Pediatric Gastroenterology, Hepatology and Nutrition
- www.Oley.org
- www.PAGER.org
- www.ThriveRx.com
- www.tubefedkids.ning.com
- www.tummytunnels.com

Made in the USA
Lexington, KY
23 September 2015